D1520040

SPOTLIGHT
ON CHILDREN'S
AUTHORS

JENNIFER L. HOLM

SUE CORBETT

Cavendish
Square

New York

Published in 2014 by Cavendish Square Publishing, LLC
303 Park Avenue South, Suite 1247, New York, NY 10010

Library of Congress Cataloging-in-Publication Data
Corbett, Sue.
Jennifer L. Holm / Sue Corbett.
p. cm.—(Spotlight on children's authors)
Includes bibliographical references and index.
Summary: "Presents the biography of children's book author Jennifer L. Holm while exploring her creative process as a writer and artist and the cultural impact of her work"—Provided by publisher.
ISBN 978-1-60870-931-1 (hardcover)—ISBN 978-1-62712-139-2 (paperback)—ISBN 978-1-60870-938-0 (ebook)
1. Holm, Jennifer L.—Juvenile literature. 2. Authors, American—21st century—Biography—Juvenile literature. 3. Children's stories—Authorship—Juvenile literature. I. Title.
PS3558.O35582Z6 2012
813'.54—dc23
[B]
2011036031

Senior Editor: Deborah Grahame-Smith
Art Director: Anahid Hamparian
Series Designer: Kay Petronio

Photo research by Linda Aveilhe
Cover photo courtesy of Jennifer L. Holm. Illustration courtesy of Matthew Holm

The photographs in this book with permission and through courtesy of:
Courtesy of Jennifer L. Holm: p. 4, 6; Copyright © 1964 by Lloyd Alexander. Courtesy Yearling Books, January 12, 1999: p. 8; Courtesy of Jennifer L. Holm: p. 10, 12; Copyright © 1999 by Jennifer L. Holm. Courtesy HarperCollins Childrens Books, a division of Harper Collins, NY: p. 15; Courtesy of Reven Wurman: p. 20; Copyright © 2001 by Jennifer L. Holm. Courtesy of Yearling, an imprint of Random House Children's Books: p. 24; Illustration copyright © 2004 by Brad Weinman. Courtesy of HarperCollins Children's Books, a division of HarperCollins Publishers: p. 27; Courtesy of Jennifer L. Holm: p. 28, 31; Copyright © 2005 by Jennifer Holm and Matthew Holm. Courtesy Random House Children's Books, a division of Random House, Inc.: p. 32; Copyright © 2006 by Jennifer Holm. Courtesy of Random House Books for Young Readers, a division of Random House, Inc.: p. 34; Courtesy of Alan Baker: p. 38; Courtesy of Jennifer L. Holm: p. 40

Printed in the United States of America

CONTENTS

The package arrived when Jenni was just a few years out of college. She was working full-time at an advertising agency in New York City and doing what she really wanted to do—write—whenever she got a chance, at night and on the weekends. Inside the package were photocopied pages from a diary written by Jenni's great-aunt, Alice Amelia Holm, whose family had emigrated from Finland to Washington Territory (Washington did not become a state until 1889) in the mid-nineteenth century.

Jenni's aunt Betty had found the diary while cleaning out the attic. It was a skinny thing—just a dozen pages containing thirteen entries over a span of seven years—but Aunt Betty thought it would make a special keepsake for her nieces and nephews. She made copies and sent one to each of them as a Christmas present.

"I think she was hoping it would show us a little bit about what life had been like," Jenni said. Jenni's father, William Holm, grew up on a farm in the same area as Great-Aunt Alice—a region once known as Little Finland because of the number of Scandinavian immigrants who had relocated on the banks of the Naselle River.

"He grew up there during the Great Depression, and he was always sharing things he called 'nickel knowledge,' random facts he knew that he said were only worth a nickel," Jenni remembered. "I never really appreciated it as a child."

The first entry in Great-Aunt Alice's diary is from 1899. She writes,

My name is
Alice Amelia Holm
And I live in Washington
On the Nasel River.
I am Twelve years of age
and will be thirteen
the 28th day of February.

Jenni read the whole diary the moment it arrived. Something about it hit her hard. Great-Aunt Alice wrote about playing tricks on her brothers, visiting cousins, and fishing on the Naselle. Suddenly, all those stories Jenni's father had told her about his boyhood in the wilds of the Pacific-swept Northwest sprang to life—in the voice of a girl not yet a teenager.

"It really struck me that here was a girl writing about what it was like to be twelve a hundred years ago," Jenni recalled. "I knew almost immediately that I wanted to write about it. In that instant, May Amelia and the Jackson family were born."

Can a photocopied document change your life?

For Jenni, it most certainly did.

Jenni visits the setting of *Our Only May Amelia*—her father's family farm in Naselle, Washington, in 2000.

Chapter 1
LITTLE MISS NEVERSTILL

Since opening that most unusual and welcome Christmas gift in 1993, **Jennifer Louise Holm** (her father called her Jenni Lou) has made the shift from writing whenever she could to writing full-time. Her novels have garnered three Newbery Honors from the American Library Association—which is like having won the Oscar for Best Supporting Actress three times—and countless state awards. With the Babymouse books, she turned a childhood love of comic books into a best-selling collaboration with her younger brother, Matthew.

This success took a lot of people by surprise, perhaps no one more so than Jenni herself. Even her mother, Beverly "Penny" Holm, would not have predicted that her only daughter would become a writer. Jenni did not start talking until she was past two years of age, because she was accustomed to having her two older brothers, Keith and Ian, wait on her.

"She would point to things and they would get it for her," Beverly recalled. "I remember Bill [Jenni's father] and I told them, 'You have to stop that. She'll get used to it.' But we also figured that once she started to talk she would never shut up and that was the truth."

The Holms were readers. Beverly said, "Everybody always had a book going. Books were a reward, something to look forward to when your work was done. So, a reader, yes. She was always a reader. But a writer?

I didn't see it," she said. "I would have guessed 'entrepreneur,' because as a little kid, she was always trying to come up with anything that could be made and sold. She painted flowers on rocks and sold them door-to-door. We called her 'Little Miss Neverstill.'"

Indeed, if Jenni had followed in her parents' footsteps, she would have gone into medicine. She was born in San Diego, at Balboa Naval Hospital, where her father was a doctor. Her parents met in the U.S. Navy when both were stationed in Oakland, California. (Her mom, the inspiration for the main character in *Penny from Heaven*, was a nurse but had to resign her navy commission when she married.) The world-famous San Diego Zoo is in the same park as the naval hospital, and Jenni feels this is significant—a harbinger of her life to come as the only girl in a family of five, sandwiched on either side by a pair of brothers. She thinks she developed a love of fantasy literature, especially Lloyd Alexander's Chronicles of Prydain, as a way of escaping from the chaotic household in which she grew up.

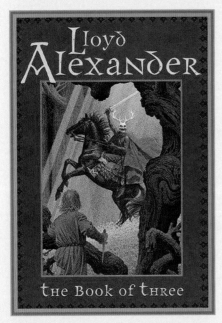

Referring to the main characters in *The Book of Three*, the first book in Alexander's series, Jenni once wrote, "I

Jenni's favorite books as a kid were Lloyd Alexander's Chronicles of Prydain series.

considered myself as beleaguered as poor Taran and Eilonwy—fighting my way through hordes of zombie-like creatures, er, I mean, boys, just to get to the bathroom," she once wrote.

Jenni's family lived briefly on Whidbey Island in Puget Sound before her father retired from the military and took a job with a pediatrics practice in Audubon, Pennsylvania. Audubon is less than 30 miles (48 kilometers) northwest of Philadelphia but worlds away from the big city. With a population of fewer than seven thousand people, it is a very small town, tucked into a curve of the Schuylkill River. The town was founded in 1823 as Shannonville, named for a large family of swine farmers. (The locals called it Hogtown.) In 1899, the town formally changed its name to honor its most famous (former) resident, naturalist painter John James Audubon, whose first home in America was on a local estate, Mill Grove, which now houses a museum dedicated to his work. It was in the fields and woods surrounding Mill Grove, a haven for wildlife, that Audubon first developed his passion for painting and drawing birds.

The Pennsylvania countryside was a source of inspiration for Jenni, too. The Holms lived on a street that ended in a cul-de-sac; a creek ran behind their property. There was only one other school-age girl on the block; the rest of the kids were boys. Along with her brothers, Keith, Ian, John, and Matt, Jenni spent a lot of time outdoors. She would climb trees and play in the creek—anything the boys did, Jenni wanted to do, too.

"I don't know if I would have called her a tomboy," said Beverly Holm. "She ran with the boys because that's who were here."

Like Babymouse, Jenni claims to have been a failure at ballet.

"The story about flunking out of ballet is true," said Beverly. "We went to one recital and there's Jenni, up onstage with her hand over her eye like an Indian scout, searching the audience for us, and then

The ballet dropout at her first (and only) dance recital in 1973.

waving and waving to make sure we saw her, while all the other girls were dancing away."

Where Jenni did excel was at school. At Audubon Elementary, she was a favorite of the librarian, Diane Ellenburg, who fed her love of fantasy novels. (A neighbor recalls that his clearest memory of Jenni as a child was once seeing her attempt to pick up leaves with a rake in one hand and a book, fanned open to the page she was trying to read, in the other.) It was Mrs. Ellenburg who introduced Jenni to the Chronicles of Prydain.

"I spent whole afternoons reading and rereading *The Book of Three*," Jenni recalled. "In fact, the highlight of a particular summer vacation was not, for me, going on the waterslide at the theme park, but stopping at a bookstore with a great kid's section and discovering—gasp!—that Mr. Alexander had written *four* more books about Taran and his friends."

By the time she was a student at Arcola Middle School, Jenni had written her first full-fledged story: "The Dragon Who Couldn't Breathe Fire," which is about a water-breathing creature who finds his calling as a firefighter. This is not the usual method, but Jenni decided to mail the story directly to Alexander, who also lived in Pennsylvania, to see if he thought it could be published.

Some time later, Jenni arrived home from school one day to learn she had a call—a "Mr. Alexander" was on the phone for her!

Alexander had not called Jenni to offer her publishing advice, however. Jenni had not included her mailing address with her manuscript—only her phone number. But her hero was on the phone! And though later she would think of "one million questions" she had for him, all she could think to say at the moment was, "I love your books!"

Alexander thanked Jenni and asked for her mailing address so that he could send her a note, which Jenni kept as a prized possession. It read as follows:

> *16 June 1981*
> *Dear Jennifer Holm:*
> *Many thanks for letting me see your story, which I'm*
> *enclosing along with this note.*
> *I enjoyed it very much; though, sad to say, I myself don't*
> *know of publishers looking for very many new manuscripts*
> *(they have more than they know what to do with!).*
> *My best suggestion is simply to keep on with your interest*
> *in writing, and—hard as it is—be patient!*
> *With warmest greetings,*
> *Lloyd Alexander*

Despite Alexander's encouragement, Jenni never considered majoring in English or becoming a writer because that didn't seem "practical," she said. "I was too intimidated to consider that. I had no clue at the time on how to become a writer."

She did love words, however. In addition to being in the marching band (though she didn't play an instrument, she became the drum majorette in her senior year) and playing lacrosse, Jenni and another student founded the debate club. The girl who didn't speak until she was more than two became a champion talker!

"She was really good," remembered Beverly. "That was her niche. In fact, because of how good she was, Bill and I, who being in medicine didn't really care for lawyers, thought that might be her calling—law."

Jenni poses with her dad, William Holm, after her 1990 graduation from Dickinson College in Carlisle, Pennsylvania.

When she graduated from high school, Jenni chose Dickinson College in Carlisle, Pennsylvania, in part because her lacrosse coach was an alumna who recommended it, and in part because it was only two hours from home. Jenni majored in international relations with the intention to become a diplomat, but nobody was hiring diplomats when, fresh out of college in 1990, she arrived in New York. Instead, she worked as a secretary for a few months before getting a job at Broadcast Arts, an animation company whose most popular show at the time was *Pee-wee's Playhouse*. For the next ten years, working in production, Jenni made short videos and, later, commercials at an advertising agency for products like Huggies baby wipes.

"Being a producer is actually not a particularly creative role. The directors, copywriters, and art directors have all the fun," Jenni said. Advertising is also a very competitive, sometimes cutthroat, business. There were many tough days when Jenni felt she would rather be doing something over which she had more control, in a less stressful environment. She began to think about what kind of job would allow her creativity to flourish without all the workplace pressure. Could she be a writer, like her hero, Lloyd Alexander? Did she have it in her?

"I had always wanted to write but I hadn't majored in English, didn't have an MFA [a master's degree in fine arts], and was very intimidated by the idea of trying to be a writer," she said. "But since I had nothing to lose, I just sort of sat down and started writing for fun."

Sequel to the Newbery Honor Book
Our Only May Amelia

the Trouble with May Amelia

jennifer l. holm

Jenni used her
memories of being
the only girl in a
large family of
boys to create May
Amelia's story.

Chapter 2
THE ROAD TO PUBLICATION

Great-Aunt Alice made only thirteen entries in her diary. Once or twice a year between 1899 and 1906, she recorded the big news of the day—for example, a wedding or the birth of a baby. In her final entry, on her birthday in 1906, she announced she had passed the exam to become a teacher and would "begin another term in the Finn country in two weeks." That's all she wrote.

So when Jenni sat down to create a novel based on Great-Aunt Alice's life, she had to use her imagination.

"I was inspired more by the idea of being a girl at that time period than the actual incidents she wrote about in her diary," Jenni said, though she did borrow a few things. Great-Aunt Alice's dog was named Bose, which Jenni changed to Bosie in her novel, *Our Only May Amelia*; Alice's "best brother" was also named Wilbert, like May Amelia's brother.

(Those who have already read *Our Only May Amelia* will be relieved to learn that in real life, baby Amy was Aunt Alice's older sister, and she lived to a ripe old age.)

But basically Jenni took her own experience as the only girl in a large family of boys and transferred it to Washington Territory at the end of the nineteenth century. She had to do a lot of research on the Chinook Indians, Finnish cooking, and the logging industry, but a fountain of knowledge about the terrain was only a phone call away: "My dad was always talking about growing up on a farm but I admit I never appreciated what he was saying until I starting writing *Our Only May Amelia*," Jenni said. "I started talking to him about his childhood and this time I took notes."

When creating May Amelia's story, Jenni chose to mimic the style of Great-Aunt Alice's diary, which is written in the first person, present tense. Great-Aunt Alice's first language was Finnish, not English, so the way she constructed sentences was not always conventional, and neither was her grammar. She randomly capitalized words, did not use quotation marks, and spoke in a way that now sounds outdated. Jenni built on this to create a unique voice for May Amelia, who, for instance, reports on her own eavesdropping by writing, "I go about fixing dinner real quiet-like so they can talk and tell secrets."

Jenni never met her Great-Aunt Alice, so she used parts of her own personality in creating spunky May Amelia, a twelve-year-old who is under pressure from her stern father to act more like a "Proper Young Lady" and less like her rambunctious brothers. (Remember, Jenni is a ballet dropout herself!) She gave May even more brothers (seven) than Jenni has herself (four). "I wanted to show that families are complicated, and that you can have very different relationships with different brothers," Jenni said.

Characters are only one element of a story; it also has to have a plot. So Jenni created lots of wilderness adventures for May Amelia. She gets herself into trouble with a bear trap, falls overboard from a boat, and saves her brothers from a cougar. "I reckon it's a Darn Good Thing I'm not a Proper Young Lady or you'd be a cougar's supper right about now,"

Ivan Alvin Wilbert Isaiah Wendell Kaarlo

Me.

CHAPTER ONE

Irritating as a Grain of Sand

My brother Wilbert tells me that I'm like the grain
of sand in an oyster. Someday I will be a Pearl, but
I will nag and irritate the poor oyster and everyone
else up until then.

Wilbert has found me here on the Baby Island
where I have to come to hide from Pappa who is Spit-
ting Mad at me. I washed out the jar of yeast starter
and we won't have bread for a week. Pappa says I'm
Just Plain Stupid because I Never Pay Attention and
that he would rather have one boy than a dozen May
Amelias because Girls Are Useless. I don't know why

Don't try this
in English class:
Jenni wrote May
Amelia's story
in the format
of a personal
diary, with lots
of incorrect
punctuation.

she tells them. Pioneer life could be very grim, but Jenni included many funny moments to balance the darker elements.

It took nearly three years to complete a draft that Jenni thought was good enough to submit to literary agents. Literary agents are the businesspeople who sell manuscripts to the editors who will publish them.

The first agent Jenni approached liked her story but thought it needed to be rewritten for a younger audience. Though Jenni's narrator was twelve, Jennis had targeted an adult audience. Uncertain about the agent's advice, Jenni asked a friend to give the manuscript to two editors she knew. They, too, said the best audience for May Amelia's story would be young readers.

Jenni listened, revised, and resubmitted to other agents. "I had a solid year of nice rejections from many, many agents before I found a lovely, wonderful agent who took me on," Jenni said. That agent, Jill Grinberg, sold the manuscript to HarperCollins.

Selling the manuscript didn't mean Jenni was done, however. Her editor, Ginee Seo, wrote lengthy letters with suggestions and comments on how the story could be improved. As Jenni told *Publishers Weekly (PW)* when the magazine gave her its Flying Start award in 1999 (special recognition for authors and illustrators who make an unusually promising debut with their first published book), "May [the character] didn't change at all, but I had originally written the book in diary format and we made it more active. The biggest change was strengthening all the brothers to give each one a well-defined character."

Those revisions were hard work, but Jenni wanted to produce the best book she possibly could. Her perseverance paid off when the book was published in June 1999 and received lots of praise from reviewers, including a starred review from *Publishers Weekly*. (A starred review means that the reviewer thinks the book is really exceptional.) *PW*'s reviewer wrote, "An unforgettable heroine narrates Holm's extraordinary debut novel." Strongly encouraging people to read the novel, the reviewer concluded, "This novel is not to be missed."

Jenni was on her way.

Jenni and her husband, Jonathan Hamel, bonded over a shared love of the *Star Wars* movies.

Chapter 3
A REAL MIRACLE!

The same month that *Our Only May Amelia* was published, another, even more important, event in Jenni's life took place: she got married!

Jenni had met Jonathan Hamel when they were both working as producers in New York City. They not only had similar jobs, but also had similar interests. They both loved comic books, reading, and *Star Wars*. (Their cat is named Princess Leia Organa.) Jenni joked that the real reason Jonathan married her was "to get my *Star Wars* bubblegum trading cards." The first song played at their wedding reception was "Cantina Band" from *Star Wars Episode IV: A New Hope*.

The couple had plenty to celebrate. The warm reception that greeted Jenni's first novel meant her editor wanted her to write more books. Before *Our Only May Amelia* had even been published, Jenni had started writing a second novel: *Boston Jane: An Adventure*, a story about a well-bred nineteenth-century young lady who travels to Oregon territory to marry her fiancé. Jenni was hard at work in early January 2000 when something extraordinary—really life changing—happened.

The Newbery Medal is the oldest award given to books written specifically for young readers, and it is perhaps the best-known children's book award in the world. Established in 1922, it was named for John

Newbery, an eighteenth-century British bookseller credited with being the first publisher of fiction designed to entertain children, rather than to instruct or to improve them. To emphasize that children deserve high-quality literature, the intent of the prize was "to encourage original creative work in the field of books for children." Responsibility for choosing the winner was assigned to the American Library Association. Each year since then, a committee of librarians reads hundreds of books in search of "the most distinguished American children's book" published that year.

Winning the Newbery Medal is about the best thing that can happen to a book. It pretty much guarantees that the audience for the book will grow exponentially. For example, school and public librarians always want to buy Newbery books, and many teachers rely on the Newbery committee's selections when they choose books for their classrooms.

In addition to the gold medal awarded to one book, the committee has always selected at least one runner-up from the titles that had lots of support among the committee members. These books, called Newbery Honor books, receive silver medallions for their covers. This is where Jenni comes in.

Early on the morning of January 17, 2000, the chairwoman of the Newbery Award Selection Committee, Carolyn Brodie, called Jenni's Brooklyn apartment and left a message. The committee had chosen *Our Only May Amelia* as a Newbery Honor book. This is the kind of phone call writers dream of getting. At the time, Jenni was in Pennsylvania, where her father, William, had been hospitalized over the weekend. Bill Holm, who had been instrumental in helping Jenni write *Our Only May Amelia*, had been diagnosed with Parkinson's disease five years earlier.

"He'd been (in the hospital) all weekend," Jenni remembered. "On that Monday, he was having a procedure done, and I was bored, so around three in the afternoon, I decided to check my voicemail. I rushed back to my room and told my mom, but she didn't believe me, so I had to play it back for her."

In the words of May Amelia, it was a real miracle!

In its citation, the Newbery Committee praised *May Amelia*'s "exuberant narration, with its unconventional punctuation," and the way in which Jenni had combined "humor and heartbreak" in her story. "May honestly lays bare her ambivalence about her brothers, who are both competitive and supportive, in this spirited novel based on the author's family history."

One of the most wonderful parts of the experience was being able to tell her dad the good news. "My dad was thrilled," Jenni remembered, "and he proceeded to tell every nurse on the ward."

Boston Jane

AN ADVENTURE

YEARLING

"Boston Jane is as fresh and fun
as a cool drink on a hot day.
I couldn't put it down."
—Meg Cabot

THE NEW YORK TIMES BESTSELLING AND
TWO-TIME NEWBERY HONOR–WINNING AUTHOR

JENNIFER L. HOLM

Jenni's second novel
follows the adventures
of a well-bred
Philadelphia girl as
she travels to Oregon
Territory in the mid-
nineteenth century.

Chapter 4
A TOUGH ACT TO FOLLOW

Winning a Newbery Honor for your first book is like hitting a home run the first time you come up to bat. No matter what you do next, unless it's another home run, it's going to seem like a bit of a letdown.

Having established herself so quickly as a gifted writer, however, Jenni felt some relief. Her editor was eager for her next book—and the ones that would come after that. *Boston Jane* grew from a stand-alone novel to a series of three books. Jenni also wrote a dark thriller, *The Creek*, and got a contract to collaborate with her husband, Jonathan, on the Stink Files, a mystery series starring a cat.

That's a lot of writing. In order to get it all done, something had to give. In 2001, Jenni quit her job in advertising to write full-time.

Just like the settings of her books—the Pacific Northwest, New Jersey, and southern Florida—Jenni's life since becoming a published author has shifted all over the American continent. As professions go, writing is among the most portable. You can pack up your laptop and files and continue your work almost anywhere.

By 2003, the Holm-Hamels were living in Maryland, where Jonathan had taken a job. In August, they welcomed their first child, Will Aaron

Hamel. Now Jenni would again have to balance her professional life with another pressing obligation: being a parent.

Jenni also had to keep coming up with ideas for stories, which, luckily for Jenni, is something she does very well. Though she had proved herself as a top-notch writer of historical fiction, she had a long-standing desire to write something completely different: a comic book.

As a kid, Jenni was a voracious consumer of comic books. After all, her four brothers (and her dad) left them strewn all over the house. She and her youngest brother, Matt, also shared a love of newspaper comic strips, like *Bloom County* and *Calvin and Hobbes*. Matt started doodling his own cartoons in junior high. "She always reminds me now that I would tack my cartoons up on my bedroom door, which was opposite her bedroom, so she was constantly faced with my artwork," said Matt, who now lives in Portland, Oregon. During college at Penn State University, Matt drew comic strips for the campus newspaper.

But one thing had always bugged Jenni about the comics she read, even her favorites: there weren't many girls in them.

"[I] was always a little annoyed that the only girl characters seemed to be Wonder Woman with her lame lasso and invisible jet, and Betty and Veronica, who mooned over some weird redheaded boy," Jenni said in an interview for BWI, a book wholesaler. "I always wanted to see a cool comic book character that girls could identify with."

Before leaving her advertising job, Jenni had come up with an idea for a female comic book hero. "I was having a really rotten day," Jenni remembered. "[W]hat we would now call a 'typical' Babymouse kind of day. Late for work, missed the bus, forgot my lunch, pouring rain, et cetera. When I got home at the end of the day, my husband saw me

Jenni and Jonathan collaborated on a mystery series starring James Edward Bristlefur, a cat.

stomping around and said, 'You are so irritable!' And the image of this irritated little mouse came into my head, with crazy whiskers, her hands on her hips, and a pink heart on her dress. I scribbled it down on a napkin and gave it to Matt the next time I saw him."

Jenni writes her novels at home after her children, Will and May, go off to school.

Chapter 5
THE MOST PROFITABLE HAND-ME-DOWN EVER

After Jenni gave Matt her scribbled image of a frazzled mouse, he started working on sketches. Matt, who is six years younger than his big sister, was also working in New York City at the time, as an editor at *Country Living* magazine. (Matt is the only Holm sibling who has a college degree in English.) He had helped Jenni on previous books by doing fact-checking and copyediting on her *Boston Jane* novels and contributing some cartoons for her illustrated book, *Middle School Is Worse Than Meatloaf*.

"We worked up something like 'A Day in the Life of Babymouse,'" Matt remembered. Their first attempt was not fully illustrated, though; it was text, interspersed with comic book–style panels every couple of pages. Matt continued, "At that time, graphic novels were autobiographical or memoir-type things, like Art Spiegelman's *MAUS*, or they were comic books, collected into book form, like The *Dark Knight* or *Watchmen*. No one was doing full graphic novels directed at young kids."

Jenni and Matt considered approaching a traditional comic book publisher, like Marvel or DC Comics, but Jenni was more comfortable in the world she already knew: book publishing. However, HarperCollins, which was publishing her novels, wasn't interested in Babymouse.

"Actually, we had no interest from anybody, initially," Matt recalled. "It was too way out in left field. It languished for a while because graphic novels for kids just weren't on anybody's radar."

That might have been the end of Babymouse, except that as Jenni was preparing to move to Maryland with Jonathan and baby Will, she decided to give away some things that Will, then nine months old, had already outgrown.

"Jenni was one of the first people I had told when I was pregnant with my first baby," remembered Shana Corey, a Random House editor who also lived in Brooklyn and had become friendly with Jenni because they traveled in the same professional circle. "I'd visited her several times after Will was born just to coo at the baby, and when they were getting ready to move to Maryland, I came over and she gave me tons of baby clothes and the newborn stroller he'd outgrown."

At the apartment that day, Jenni showed Shana the Babymouse sketches and told her she'd pitched the idea of a comic book about the character to several publishers without success. "I loved the Babymouse doodle, and I thought it could be really fun to work with Jenni, so I said, 'Well, why don't you pitch it to me?'" Shana said.

Soon afterward, Jenni went into Random House's office, explained how she had longed for a comic book starring a girl when she'd been a kid, and said that her brother was an accomplished illustrator. She showed them the material they'd worked up about a mouse who lives in her imagination and longs for excitement, stardom, and travel, but deals with dodgeball, a crammed locker, and a mean girl, Felicia Furrypaws, who revels in taking Babymouse down a notch every chance she gets.

"Shana said, 'We love it. Let's do it,'" Matt remembered. "It wasn't just that they accepted our idea, which was great, it was that they

Jenni has relied on her brother Matt for copyediting, research help, and providing ideas and artwork for their Babymouse series.

were incredibly enthusiastic. That was really important because none of us really knew what we were doing. We were going to have to figure it out together."

"Sometimes," Shana said, "it's actually better when you are trying to get approval to acquire a manuscript if no one has done it before. It certainly helped in this case."

More than 1.5 million books later, it's clear there was a young audience for graphic novels. There are now more than fifteen books in the Babymouse series, and more are on the way. Each installment starts with Jenni and Matt brainstorming on a particular topic—for instance, Babymouse going to camp, dreaming of being a rock star, or getting a puppy. "Jenni might say, 'Okay, how about a book where Babymouse

Jenni's inspiration for the character of Babymouse came during one of those days when nothing goes right.

goes to the beach on summer vacation?' Then we each rattle off as many anecdotes and funny things as we can remember from our many trips to the Jersey Shore as kids, and Jenni goes and writes the manuscript," Matt said.

Jenni writes a script in the storyboard format she used as a producer of TV commercials. The storyboard breaks out each scene into a panel with separate rows for narration, dialogue, and a description of the setting and physical action. Matt reads Jenni's script and makes suggestions, and then they send the script to Shana, who makes more suggestions. Once the manuscript is approved, Matt starts drawing small thumbnail sketches for every scene in the book, and he scans them into his computer so he can e-mail them to Jenni. The back-and-forth continues until everybody agrees on the words, illustrations, and layout. Then, using a Wacom drawing tablet attached to a computer, Matt draws the final inks (images) for the book.

"And, of course, I add the pink," he said.

Though there hadn't been any graphic novels for kids at the time Jenni and Matt were dreaming up Babymouse, the first book, *Babymouse: Queen of the World!*, was greeted enthusiastically. "Graphic novels for the early elementary set are rare, and this humorous and adventurous series will be snapped up," read one review in the *Bulletin of the Center for Children's Books*. Many people credit the Babymouse series and Jeff Smith's Bone series, which was also published in book form in 2005, with jump-starting a comic book renaissance among kids.

In 2011, Jenni and Matt began a new graphic novel series, Squish, about a comic-book-loving amoeba. Since then four books in the Squish series have been published, with more to come.

"To think, it all started with Jenni giving me that stroller," Shana said.

JENNIFER L. HOLM

Newbery Honor-Winning Author of
OUR ONLY MAY AMELIA

Penny
FROM HEAVEN

Jenni's second
Newbery Honor-
winning novel
was based on her
mother's childhood
in New Jersey.

Chapter 6
A STORY IDEA FROM HEAVEN

To keep the family peace, if you write an award-winning novel about your father's side of the family, you'd better be prepared to write one about your mom's side, too. This is just what Jenni did when she wrote *Penny from Heaven*.

"She was looking for an idea, and I think she realized that she had a lot of material with all the things I had told her about growing up in Red Bank [New Jersey], and my adventures with my cousin Henry, who was two years older than me," said Jenni's mom, the Penny of the book's title.

Beverly Ann "Penny" Scaccia grew up in a large family of Italian Americans during World War II, when the United States was at war with Italy, which had aligned itself with Nazi Germany. Her father died tragically in the months before she was born. Like the hero of Jenni's novel, she is told she was nicknamed Penny because one of her father's favorite songs was "Pennies from Heaven," sung by Bing Crosby.

"I went down to where she was living in Maryland," recalled Jenni's mom, "and we sat on her little patio and she interviewed me. She also made a lot of stuff up because that's what you have to do. There was enough there for a book, that's for sure."

In a process that has become her specialty, Jenni took elements from her mother's childhood, combined them with thorough research, and wove a funny and poignant coming-of-age tale about a girl growing up without her father, but among his eccentric and lovable clan during an era when discrimination against Italian Americans was prevalent. Penny and her cousin, Frankie, get into lots of humorous trouble but there's a serious side to the story, too, as Penny tries to get the two sides of her family to talk about her the mystery surrounding her father's death at a young age.

According to Shana Corey, what makes Jenni's stories work for today's young readers is that the characters feel real: "Jenni's characters never feel like you are viewing them through a soft-focus lens, like they were characters in a black-and-white movie. These are flesh-and-blood kids who happen to live in the 1930s or the 1950s," she said.

Another distinctive element of Jenni's work is that although historical fiction does not typically attract a lot of boy readers, her novels are full of humor as well as blood and guts, which do tend to attract boys. People bleed and lose limbs; eyes are put out; babies die. Maybe it's the fact that Jenni grew up with four brothers, but she generally does not prettify the way things are. "She doesn't have a prissy bone in her body," Corey said.

As the daughter of a doctor and a nurse, Jenni heard all about the hard facts of human frailty, even around the kitchen table. "Anybody that's in that profession, it's so part of your life, there is no mystique about it," said Penny Holm. "Bill would sometimes have go out two to three times a night, and we'd hear all about what he'd seen in the morning, though, of course, he never mentioned anyone's name," she recalled.

Another facet of Jenni's novels that reviewers have cited is that although she has clearly done her homework about the period in which they are set, her stories wear their research very lightly. "She works the details in so subtly, you don't even notice that it is research," Corey said.

Finally, one of the best aspects of working with Jenni, Corey said, is that she is not only willing but also eager to revise her manuscript. "She's an avid reviser, and she will say to me, 'Be brutal,'" Corey said. "She encourages me to be as critical as I can because she wants it to be good."

Penny from Heaven was published by Random House in July 2006. On a cold morning in January 2007, it was snowing in Maryland and Will's preschool had been canceled, so he wanted to play in the snow. After Jenni got him all suited up she realized that Princess Leia (the cat) was nowhere to be seen. Since Princess Leia was an indoor cat, this concerned her greatly, so she suited up herself and went on a massive hunt for her lost cat.

Meanwhile, the chairperson of the Newbery Award Selection Committee was leaving a message on Jenni's answering machine: *Penny from Heaven* had been chosen as a Newbery Honor book.

"I missed the call again!" Jenni said.

Princess Leia was found, much later, sleeping on a heating grate inside.

Jenni is a frequent guest at schools,
book festivals, and writers' conferences.

Chapter 7
WHAT'S NEXT FOR JENNI?

Jenni and Jonathan now live in California, in a suburb of San Francisco. In 2007, their family grew with the addition of Millie May, born just in time to see her mother collect her Newbery Honor at the American Library Association annual conference in Washington, D.C.

Jenni continues to write every day. She and brother Matt have contracts for more installments in the Babymouse series, and they have to keep coming up with ideas for their new cartoon character, Squish, the amoeba.

For Jenni, the future holds an ongoing juggling act—meeting manuscript deadlines, visiting schools, writing speeches, accepting awards—all of which she'll mix with the responsibilities of motherhood. It's a good thing it seems like Millie has inherited her mother's sense of humor. Jenni posted this on Facebook one day in 2011: "I went to Millie's pre-K to talk about being a writer today. Kids are on rug and I say, 'Does anyone know what I do?' Millie shouts out: 'Fold laundry!' (Cue teachers snorting.) Typical."

In 2010, Jenni published another novel of historical fiction, *Turtle in Paradise*, a story inspired by her mother's grandmother, called Nana, who grew up in Key West, Florida, during the Great Depression.

Jenni's third Newbery Honor-winning novel was inspired by her great-grandmother Jennie Lewin Peck (far right), who emigrated from the Bahamas to Key West in the late 1800s. She is shown here with her husband, Ernest Peck, and Penny Holm (center), Jenni's mom.

Nana was a Conch, which is what emigrants from the Bahamas who settled in the Florida Keys called themselves.

Jenni said, "During the summers, Nana would take my mom to Key West to visit relatives. My mom didn't really like going. . . . It was hot, people didn't have air conditioners like they do now, and strange. (She was given avocado on Cuban bread for breakfast instead of pancakes.) And then there was the wacky warning that she should 'shake out her shoes' every morning. My mom thought this was an oddball superstition until one morning when she shook her shoes and out popped . . . a scorpion! When my editor, Shana Corey, started asking me about my Key West family, I just knew that there was a story in there somewhere."

The story Jenni came up with is about Turtle, who is eleven when her mother ships her off, alone, to live with her aunt in Key West. Aunt Minnie can barely conceal her disgust with being delivered another mouth to feed, and her cousins and their friends (boys with nicknames like Beans, Pork Chop, and Termite) do not welcome Turtle with open arms either. Like Jenni's mom in real life, Turtle finds Key West mighty strange and downright unfriendly. Her cousins' Diaper Gang, which takes care of fussy babies, won't let her join (no girls allowed) until Turtle uncovers a treasure map, which she hopes will put her on Easy Street (like in *Little Orphan Annie*) and allow her mother to give up her housecleaning job in New Jersey.

Turtle in Paradise, released in May 2010, received starred reviews in *Publishers Weekly*, *Kirkus Reviews,* and *Booklist*, which called the story a "hilarious blend of family dramas seasoned with a dollop of adventure."

On a mild morning in January 2011, Jenni was walking Will to school when the phone rang at home.

She missed the call again. *Turtle in Paradise* had been named a Newbery Honor book.

JENNI LIKES TO READ:

As a kid, Jenni devoured books and, boy, has there been a payoff! She doesn't think she ever would have become a writer if she hadn't been a reader first. She loved comic books, but she also loved fantasy novels, especially those by fellow Pennsylvanian Lloyd Alexander. You'll find some of these books, her favorites, in your school or public library.

Lloyd Alexander's Chronicles of Prydain series:

The Book of Three

The Black Cauldron

The Castle of Llyr

Taran Wanderer

The High King

The Boxcar Children, a series by Gertrude Chandler Warner

Calvin & Hobbes books by Bill Watterson

Prince Valiant, collected comic strips by Hal Foster

WE3 by Grant Morrison, a graphic novel for teenagers

The Xanth series by Piers Anthony

BOOKS BY JENNIFER L. HOLM

Our Only May Amelia (HarperCollins, 1999)

Boston Jane: An Adventure (HarperCollins, 2001)

Boston Jane: Wilderness Days (HarperCollins, 2002)

The Creek (HarperCollins, 2003)

Boston Jane: The Claim (HarperCollins, 2004)

The Stink Files, written with Jonathan Hamel (HarperCollins, 2004, 2005)

Penny from Heaven (Random House, 2006)

Middle School Is Worse Than Meatloaf: A Year Told Through Stuff (Atheneum, 2007)

Turtle in Paradise (Random House, 2010)

The Trouble with May Amelia (Atheneum, 2011)

Graphic Novels with Matthew Holm

The Babymouse series (multiple titles) (Random House, 2005–)

Squish: Super Amoeba (multiple titles) (Random House, 2011–)

GLOSSARY

alumna—A female graduate or former student of a school, college, or university.

ambivalence—An emotion caused by having two opposing ideas or feelings about something at the same time.

anecdotes—Short personal accounts of an incident or event.

beleaguered—Feeling under siege, annoyed, or under pressure.

conventional—Following socially accepted customs of behavior or style, especially in a way that lacks imagination.

cutthroat—Aggressive and merciless in striving for supremacy.

entrepreneur—A risk-taking businessperson who initiates his or her own independent ventures.

exponentially—In a way that increases at a higher and higher rate.

graphic novel—A novel-length story told in a comic book format.

languished—Was neglected or forgotten.

Nazi Germany—A reference to the period of German history after Adolf Hitler came to power in 1933.

niche—A specialized activity, market, or area of expertise that suits someone's talents or personality.

Parkinson's disease—A continuously worsening nervous disorder, often marked by symptoms of trembling hands, monotone voice, and a slow, shuffling walk.

pediatrics—The branch of medicine concerned with the care and development of children.

revels—Takes great pleasure.

soft-focus lens—A film-camera accessory that produces a slight blurring of a photograph or a filmed image, thus giving it a hazy appearance, in order to achieve a special effect such as romance or nostalgia.

voracious—Unusually eager or enthusiastic.

CHRONOLOGY

June 16, 1968: Jenni is born in San Diego, California.

Spring 1981: Jenni sends a copy of her story "The Dragon Who Couldn't Breathe Fire" to Newbery medalist Lloyd Alexander.

June 1986: Jenni graduates from Methacton High School in Eagleville, Pennsylvania.

June 1990: Jenni graduates from Dickinson College with a degree in international studies. She moves to Queens, New York, and takes a job as a secretary before landing a job at Broadcast Arts, an animation company.

December 1993: Jenni receives a photocopy of Great-Aunt Alice Amelia's diary as a Christmas present from her father's sister, Elizabeth Holm.

May 1999: Jenni is married to Jonathan Hamel.

May 28, 1999 (the next day): Jenni's first book, *Our Only May Amelia*, is published.

January 17, 2000: *Our Only May Amelia* wins a Newbery Honor Award from the American Library Association.

January 22, 2007: *Penny from Heaven* wins a Newbery Honor.

January 10, 2011: *Turtle in Paradise* wins a Newbery Honor.

FURTHER INFORMATION

Books

Are you interested in trying to write stories yourself? These two books offer guidance:

Levine, Gail Carson. *Writing Magic*. New York: Collins, 2006.

Messner, Kate. *Real Revision: Authors' Strategies to Share with Student Writers*. Portland, ME: Stenhouse, 2011.

Websites

www.jenniferholm.com

www.matthewholm.net

BIBLIOGRAPHY

A note to report writers from Sue Corbett

To write this biography, I read all of Jenni's wonderful books and did extensive research online. I read all the articles that other journalists had written about her. I had interviewed Jenni myself years ago, in my role as the children's book reviewer for the *Miami Herald,* but after I had compiled a list of questions that my research hadn't answered, I interviewed Jenni again. I also spoke to her editors; her mom, Beverly "Penny" Holm; her brother and collaborator, Matthew Holm; former teachers; booksellers; and librarians.

Below is a list of sources I used to write this biography. Any time *you* write a report, you should also keep track of where you found your information. It is fine to use information in your report if you found it somewhere else, as long as you attribute it—that is, as long as you say where you got the information and give the source credit in a footnote, endnote, or note within the report itself. (Your teacher can tell you how he or she prefers you to list your sources.)

It is never okay to pass off other people's work as your own.

PRINT ARTICLES

"Author Jennifer Holm Finds Inspiration in Quirky Family Tales," by Jessica Harrison, *The Deseret News,* May 9, 2010.

"Flying Start: Jennifer Holm," by Ingrid Roper, *Publishers Weekly*, June 28, 1999, pp. 28–29.

"Growing Up Weird," by Jennifer Holm. IndieBound.org, 2008. Accessible at http://www.indiebound.org/author-interviews/holmjennifer.

"Interview: Jennifer and Matthew Holm." BWI *TitleTale*s, no author given, 2009. Accessible at http://bwibooks.com/articles/holm-holm.php.

"Winner Interview Series: Jennifer L. Holm, 2011 Golden Kite Award for Fiction," by Alice Pope, SCBWI Children's Market Blog, March 29, 2011. Accessible at http://scbwi.blogspot.com/2011/03/winner-interivew-series-jennifer-l-holm.html.

INTERVIEWS

(All interviews were conducted by Sue Corbett.)
Interview with Jennifer L. Holm, Miami Beach, Florida, November 20, 2010.
Telephone interview with Beverly "Penny" Holm, March 18, 2011.
Telephone interview with Shana Corey, Random House editor, March 18, 2011.
Telephone interview with Matthew Holm, April 1, 2011.

INDEX

ABOUT THE AUTHOR:

Sue Corbett is a reporter who has worked for the *Miami Herald*, *People* magazine, and *Publishers Weekly*. She is also the author of several novels for kids, including *The Last Newspaper Boy in America*, *Free Baseball*, and *12 Again*.